Ladybird Readers

School Trip

Series Editor: Sorrel Pitts
Text adapted by Sorrel Pitts
Song lyrics by Pippa Mayfield

LADYBIRD BOOKS

UK | USA | Canada | Ireland | Australia
India | New Zealand | South Africa

Ladybird Books is part of the Penguin Random House group of companies
whose addresses can be found at global.penguinrandomhouse.com.
www.penguin.co.uk   www.puffin.co.uk   www.ladybird.co.uk

Text adapted from *Peppa Pig: School Bus Trip*, first published by Ladybird Books, 2008
This version first published by Ladybird Books, 2017
Updated version reprinted 2022
005

Printed in China

The authorized representative in the EEA is Penguin Random House Ireland,
Morrison Chambers, 32 Nassau Street, Dublin D02 YH68

A CIP catalogue record for this book is available from the British Library

ISBN: 978-0-241-28372-1

All correspondence to:
Ladybird Books
Penguin Random House Children's
One Embassy Gardens, 8 Viaduct Gardens, London SW11 7BW

MIX
Paper from
responsible sources
FSC® C018179

School Trip

Based on the Peppa Pig
TV series

Picture words

Peppa

Madame
Gazelle

mountain

echo

picnic

Peppa and her friends went on a school trip.

"Are you all here?" said Madame Gazelle.

"Yes," they said.

The children loved school trips.

"Where are we going?"
said Peppa.

"We are going to the
mountains," said
Madame Gazelle.

"Great!" said Peppa
and her friends.

9

The bus went up a big mountain.

"Go, bus, go!" said Peppa.

The bus went up and up.

The children sang a song!

The bus stopped at the top of the mountain. Peppa and her friends stood on the grass.

"Look! What big mountains!"
said Madame Gazelle.

Peppa could see lots of mountains and lots of snow.

"Wow!" she said.

Then, the children heard, "Wow! Wow! Wow!"

Wow! Wow!

"What was that noise?" said Peppa.

"That was an echo," said Madame Gazelle. "You often hear echoes in the mountains. You spoke, and your words made an echo."

"We can do that again!" said Peppa. "Let's all make an echo."

"Wow!" the children said.

"Wow!" they heard.
"Wow! Wow! Wow!"

Peppa and her friends
loved the echoes.

Wow! Wow! Wow! Wow!

"Are you hungry, children?"
said Madame Gazelle.
"I have got a big picnic."

"Great!" said the children.

"Where are the ducks?"
said Peppa.

Peppa and her friends
waited for the ducks.

Then, they saw the ducks!

"Great!" said Peppa.

"Quack! Quack! Quack!"
said the ducks.

"Come here, ducks,"
said Madame Gazelle.

"Yes, come to our picnic,
ducks," said Peppa.

And the ducks had a big
picnic, too.

"We must go back to school now," said Madame Gazelle.

The children sat in the bus. The bus went down the mountain.

The children sang a song.
Peppa and her friends love
school trips!

Activities

The key below describes the skills
practiced in each activity.

🖊 Spelling and writing

📖 Reading

💬 Speaking

❓ Critical thinking

✿ Preparation for the Cambridge
Young Learners Exams

1 Look and read. Put a ✓ or a ✗ in the boxes. 📖 ⬡

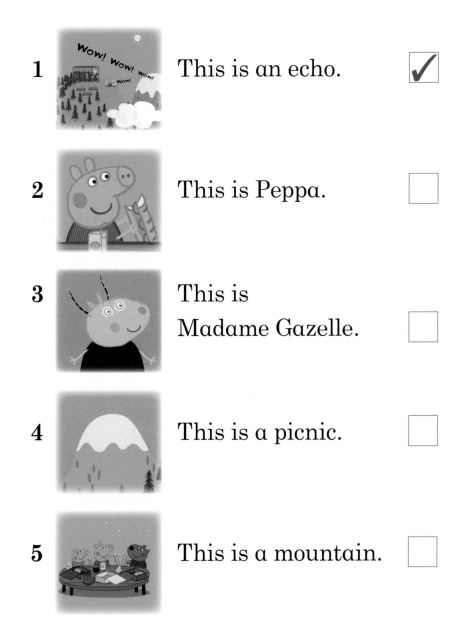

1   This is an echo.   ✓

2   This is Peppa.   ☐

3   This is Madame Gazelle.   ☐

4   This is a picnic.   ☐

5   This is a mountain.   ☐

2 **Look and read. Write *yes* or *no*.**

Peppa and her friends went on a school trip.

"Are you all here?" said Madame Gazelle.

"Yes," they said.

The children loved school trips.

6   7

1 Peppa and her friends went on a school trip.   yes

2 Madame Gazelle went on the school trip.   ....

3 Peppa and her friends did not like school trips.   ....

4 All the children were there.   ....

5 The children went on the school trip in a car.   ....

3 Find the words.

ohdmountaintidbuseolmpicnicwotihMadameGazelleiPeppatducksk

mountain
ducks
Madame Gazelle
bus
picnic
Peppa

4 **Ask and answer questions about the picture with a friend.** 💬

"Where are we going?" said Peppa.

"We are going to the mountains," said Madame Gazelle.

"Great!" said Peppa and her friends.

1 *Where is Madame Gazelle?*

She is in front of the children.

2 Where is Peppa?

3 Where is the bus going?

4 What does Peppa say?

5 Look at the picture and read the questions. Write the answers using the words in the box. 📖 ✏️

The bus went up a big mountain.

"Go, bus, go!" said Peppa.

The bus went up and up.

The children sang a song!

> go
>
> on
>
> up
>
> up and up

1 Where were the children?

They were ___on___ the bus.

2 Where did they go?

They went _____ a big mountain.

3 What did Peppa say?

"Go, bus,_____!" said Peppa.

4 Where did the bus go?

The bus went _____.

6 **Match the two parts of the sentences.**

The bus stopped at the top of the mountain. Peppa and her friends stood on the grass.

"Look! What big mountains!" said Madame Gazelle.

12   13

1 The bus went

2 The bus stopped

3 Peppa and her friends stood

4 "Look!"

5 "What big

a on the grass.

b up and up.

c said Madame Gazelle.

d mountains!"

e at the top of the mountain.

7 Circle the correct words.

1
  a bus
  b school

2
  a ducks
  b children

3
  a up
  b down

4
  a picnic
  b mountain

37

8 Circle the correct pictures.

1 Who likes school trips?

 (a) (b)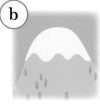

2 Where did they go?

(a)  (b)

3 "What was that noise?" said Peppa.

(a)  (b)

4 What said "Quack! Quack! Quack!"?

(a)  (b)

9 Circle the correct words.

1 **What** / **Who** did Peppa say?

2 **Who** / **Where** drove the bus?

3 **Who** / **What** did Madame Gazelle say?

4 **Where** / **Who** do you hear echoes?

5 **Who** / **Where** likes picnics?

10 Work with a friend. You are in the mountains. Say these words and your friend makes the echo.

1

> *Wow!*

> *Wow! Wow! Wow!*

2 Echo!

3 Great!

4 Snow!

5 Peppa!

11 Order the story. Write 1—5. 📖

_____ "Let's all make an echo," said Peppa.

_____ "Wow!" the children said.

___1___ "We can do that again!" said Peppa.

_____ Peppa and her friends loved the echoes.

_____ "Wow!" they heard. "Wow! Wow! Wow!"

12 Who said this?

| Madame Gazelle | Peppa | the children | the ducks |

1 "Are you hungry, children?"

said ___Madame Gazelle___.

2 "Great!"

said _____.

3 "Where are our friends?"

said _____.

4 "Quack! Quack! Quack!"

said _____.

13 Look at the letters. Write the words.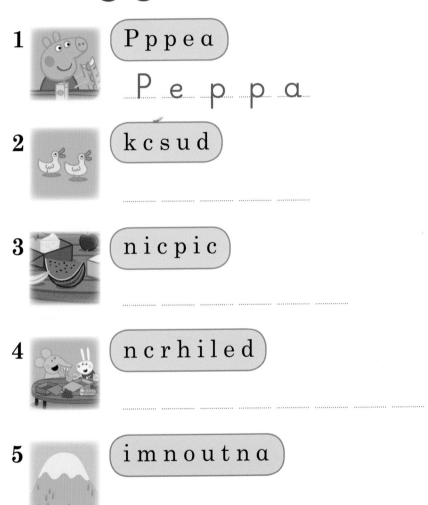

1   P p p e a

    P e p p a

2   k c s u d

....

3   n i c p i c

....

4   n c r h i l e d

....

5   i m n o u t n a

....

14 Ask and answer *Do you like?* questions with a friend.

1 ducks

> Do you like ducks?

> Yes, I do!

2 sandwiches

3 picnics

4 school trips

5 apples

15 Do the crossword.

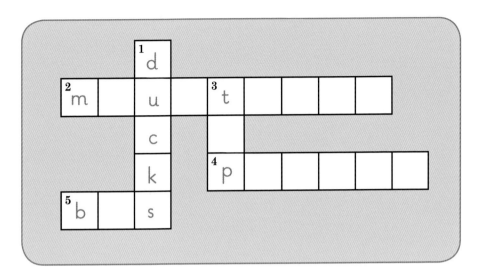

Down

1 These animals say, "Quack! Quack! Quack!"

3 The bus stopped at the . . . of the mountain.

Across

2 Peppa and her friends went to the . . .

4 Madame Gazelle had a big . . . for the children.

5 The children went on a school trip in a . . .

16 **Talk to your friend about school trips. Answer the questions.** 💬 ❓

1 Would you like to
go on a school trip?

Yes, I would.

2 Would you like to go to the mountains?
Why? / Why not?

3 Would you like to make echoes
with your friends?

4 Would you like to have a picnic
with your friends?

17 **Read the questions. Write the answers.** 📖 ✏️

1 Did Peppa and her friends have food for the ducks?

<u>Yes, they did.</u>

2 Were the ducks blue?

3 Did Madame Gazelle watch the ducks?

4 How many ducks were there?

Level 2

The Gingerbread Man	**Sly Fox and Red Hen**	**The Monster Next Door**	**Wild Animals**	**Little Red Riding Hood**
978-0-241-25442-4	978-0-241-25443-1	978-0-241-25444-8	978-0-241-25445-5	978-0-241-25446-2
Dinosaurs	**Topsy and Tim The Big Race**	**Goes to the Treehouse**	**Sports Day**	**Going on a Picnic**
978-0-241-25447-9	978-0-241-25448-6	978-0-241-25449-3	978-0-241-26222-1	978-0-241-26221-4
Peter Rabbit and the Angry Owl	**Superhero Max**	**We Can Help!**	**School Trip**	**Daddy Pig's New Van**
978–0–241–28369–1	978–0–241–28368–4	978–0–241–28367–7	978–0–241–28372–1	978–0–241–28371–4

Now you're ready for Level 3!